RONALD SEARLE'S

NON-SEXIST DICTIONARY

SOUVENIR PRESS

Typeset, printed and bound in Great Britain by
Hazell Watson & Viney Limited
Member of BPCC plc
Aylesbury, Bucks, England

Although I am the last person on this shaky planet to dream of being cast in the non-bleating rôle of a sacrificial lamb sandwiched between the choppers of the Machos and the Amazons, I do realise that I am on more than delicate ground with a subject such as this. But the time does seem to have come for exercising the de-sexerciser or, at least, for having a second look at some of the more sombre sexist crannies of the English language.

Unisex can go far in French, for example. Who, I wonder, was responsible for the decision that *la barbe* should be a feminine word? It could be, of course, that way back before everybody was in trousers, stubble also flourished regardless of gender. To this day, nobody seems to mind. But in our neuter English, there are some nasty anomalies that cry out for correction. Is it logic that men should monopolise 'menopause'? Out of justice, 'womenopause' must come.

This little book is a timid footstep towards the establishment of a first slightly less sexist dictionary. Recowomend it to your friends!

R.S.

Abandonment — Abandonwoment

Abdomen — Abdowomen

Accomplishment — Accomplishwoment

Achievement — Achievewoment

Acknowledgement — Acknowledgewoment

Acumen — Acuwomen

Achievewoment

Agreement — Agreewoment

Amend — Awomend

Amenity — Awomenity

Apartment — Apartwoment

Argument — Arguwoment

Ballad — Ballass

Bohemian — Boshemian

Boisterous — Goilsterous

Boycott — Girlcott

Arguwoment

Buoy — Guoyl

Clementine — Clewomentine

Commando — Cowomando

Commendation — Cowomendation

Commentator — Cowomentator

Compartment — Compartwoment

Compliment — Compliwoment

Demented — Dewomented

Dénouement — Dénouewoment

Department — Departwoment

Detachment — Detachwoment

Detriment — Detriwoment

Development — Developwoment

Devilment — Devilwoment

Dimensions — Diwomensions

Dismantle — Diswomantle

Dolman — Dolwoman

Dormant — Dorwomant

Developwoment

Egomania — Egowomania

Elementary — Elewomentary

Emanate — Ewomanate

Emancipate — Ewomancipate

Employment — Employwoment

Encampment — Encampwoment

Engagement — Engagewoment

Elewomentary

Entanglement — Entanglewoment

Entanglewoment

Entertainment — Entertainwoment

Environment — Environwoment

Erotomania — Erotowomania

Excrement — Excrewoment

Experiment — Experiwoment

Experiwoment

Ferment — Ferwoment

Fitment — Fitwoment

Foment — Fowoment

Fragment — Fragwoment

Fragwoment

Gamesmanship — Gameswomanship

German — Gerwoman

Gourmandise — Gourwomandise

Gourwomandise

Hedonist — Shedonist

Heretic — Himetic

Himalayas — Heralayas

Historian — Hertorian

Histrionic — Hertrionic

Hogmanay — Hogwomanay

Homicide — Lesbicide

Human — Huwoman

Hymen — Hywomen

Heralayas

Hymn — Hermn

Hermn

Immanent — Imwomanent

Immense — Imwomense

Impediment — Impediwoment

Implement — Implewoment

Improvement — Improvewoment

Inhuman — Inhuwoman

Inhuwoman

Instrument — Instruwoment

Interment — Interwoment

Investment — Investwoment

Involvement — Involvewoment

Jerrymander — Jerrywomander

Judgement — Judgewoment

Instruwoment

Lamentable — Lawomentable

Liniment — Liniwoment

Manacles — Womanacles

Manager — Womanager

Manchester — Womanchester

Womanacles

Manfully — Womanfully

Manger — Womanger

Mangle — Womangle

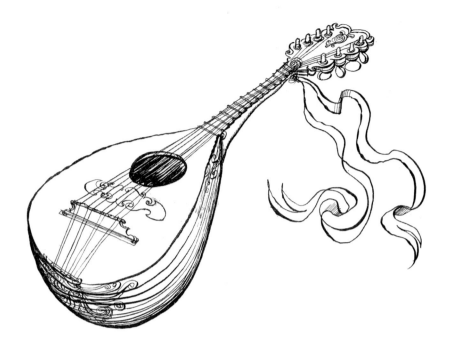

Mandolin

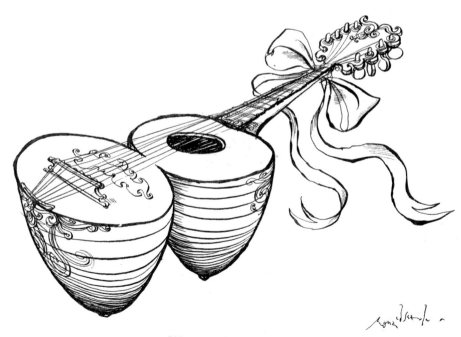

Womandolin

Mangy — Womangy

Manhandle — Womanhandle

Manhattan — Womanhattan

Manhole — Womanhole

Womanhole

Mango — Womango

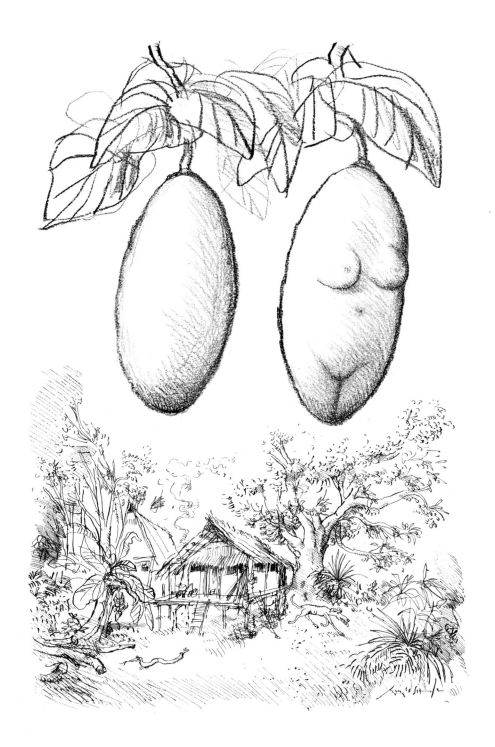

Maniac — Womaniac

Manicure — Womanicure

Manifestation — Womanifestation

Manipulate — Womanipulate

Mannequin — Womannequin

Manoeuvre — Womanoeuvre

Mansion — Womansion

Womaniac

Manslaughter — Womanslaughter

Mantis — Womantis

Manuel — Womanuel

Manufacture — Womanufacture

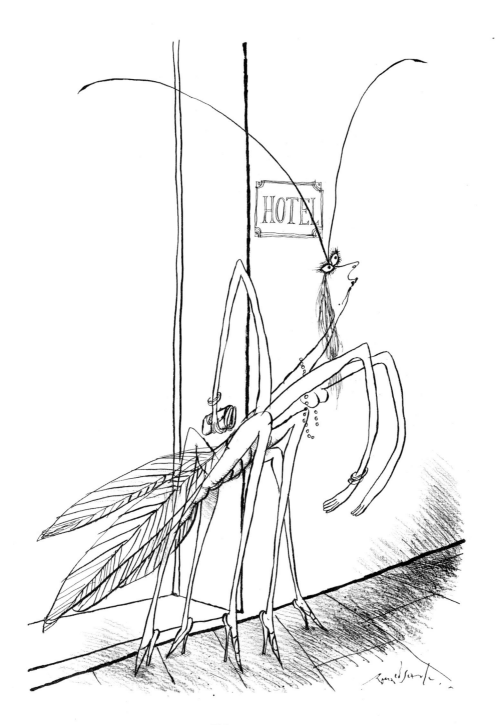

Womantis

Manure — Womanure

Manuscript — Womanuscript

Menace — Womenace

Womenace

Menagerie — Womenagerie

Mending — Womending

Menhir — Womenhir

Menial — Womenial

Menopause — Womenopause

Womenagerie

Menstrual — Womenstrual

Mention — Womention

Mentality — Womentality

Menu — Womenu

Nomenclature — Nowomenclature

Omen — Owomen

Ornament — Ornawoment

Ornawoment

Ottoman — Ottowoman

Outmanoeuvre — Outwomanoeuvre

Overmantel — Overwomantel

Outwomanoeuvre

Parliament — Parliawoment

Payment — Paywoment

Pediment — Pediwoment

Permanent — Perwomanent

Permanganate — Perwomanganate

Pediwoment

Phenomenal — Phenowomenal

Pomander — Powomander

Presentment — Presentwoment

Promenade — Prowomenade

Pullman — Pullwoman

Punishment — Punishwoment

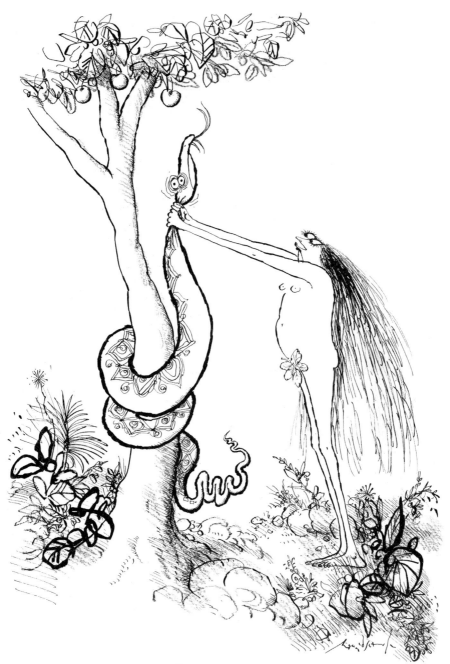

Punishwoment

Salamander — Salawomander

Semen — Sewomen

Superhuman — Superhuwoman

Supplement — Supplewoment

Supplewoment

Tournament — Tournawoment

Tournawoment

Undermanned — Underwomanned

Unmanageable — Unwomanageable

Vehement — Vehewoment

Vestments — Vestwoments

Vestwoments

Womanize — Manize

Manize

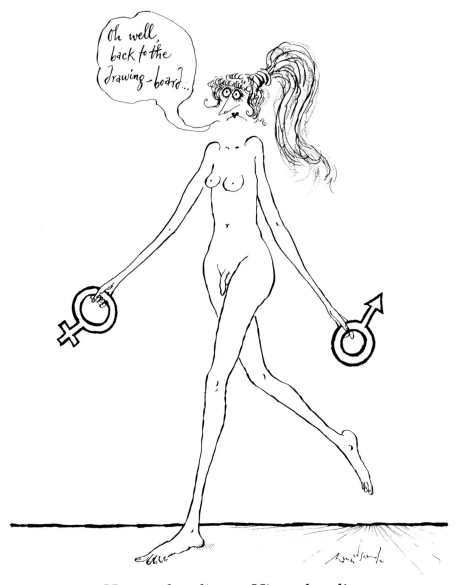

Hermaphrodite — Himaphrodite